AMAZONIAN CANOPY: THE ROOF OF THE WORLD'S RAINFOREST

Northwater

CONSTANTINE ISSIGHOS

Copyright 2012 © Constantine Issighos. Published in Canada. Printed in U.S.A. No part of this book may be reproduced or transmitted in any form or by any means, electronic or mechanical, including photocopying, recording, and/or by any information storage and retrieval system except by a reviewer who may quote brief passages in a review to be printed in a magazine, newspaper, or on the web without written permission in writing from the author/publisher. For information, please contact www.awaqkunabooks.com

NorthWater is an imprint of Awaqkuna Books Inc.

Vol. 10 of THE AMAZON EXPLORATION SERIES:
AMAZONIAN CANOPY:
THE ROOF OF THE WORLD'S RAINFOREST

Library and Archives Canada

ISBN 978-0-9878599-9-0

Library and Archives Canada Cataloguing in Publication

ATTENTION CHILDRENS ASSOCIATIONS, BOOK STORES, PUBLIC OR PRIVATE LIBRARIES: quantity discounts are available on bulk purchases of this book series.

THE AMAZON EXPLORATION SERIES

Children's Books
by
Constantine Issighos

1. Upper Amazon Voyage by River Boat
2. The People of the River
3. The Children of the River
4. Amazon's Nature of Things
5. Echoes of Nature: a Beautiful Wild Habitat
6. The Amazon Rainforest
7. Amazonian Sisterhood
8. Amazon River Wolves
9. Amazonian Landscapes and Sunsets
10. Amazonian Canopy: the Roof of the World's Rainforest
11. Amazonian Tribes: a World of Difference
12. Birds and Butterflies of the Amazon
13. The Great Wonders of the Amazon
14. The Jaguar People
15. The Fresh Water Giants
16. The Call of the Shaman
17. Indigenous Families: Life in Harmony with Nature
18. Amazon in Peril
19. Giant Tarantulas and Centipedes
20. The Amazon Ethno-Botanical Garden
21. The Real Amazon Tribal Warriors

The Amazon rainforest is a tropical woodland with lush vegetation and great biological diversity. There are three layers to the rainforest; the canopy, the understory, and the forest floor. The canopy is the top part of the giant trees whose inhabitants includes monkeys, giant spiders and birds such as toucans, parrots, parakeets and turquoise tanagers. The understory is where snakes, frogs, and lizards live. The decomposers live on the forest floor, along with jaguars, anteaters, tapirs and other large animals.

Some species are born, live and die in one of these tree layers, without ever moving from one level of the rainforest to another. There are more species of plants and animals living in the rainforest than the entire world's other biospheres combined. It is estimated that more than 350 bird species, more than 80,000 plant species and 30 million animal species, most of them insects, live in the Amazon rainforest.

The rainforest covering the Amazon basin looks from the air as a uniform green carpet cut here and there by the Amazon River and its hundreds of tributaries. Actually, the forest is anything but uniform. The so-called "carpet" is a forest canopy formed by broad leaves of many different kinds of giant trees, most reaching more than 60 meters (200 feet) high.

It is difficult to determine the age of tropical trees because they do not have easily identified annual rings and they grow so slowly. The slow rate is likely due to the poor nutrient content of the soil of the Amazon basin combined with the low light conditions created by the shade of the forest canopy. However, trees in the Amazon rainforest are older than originally believed by scientists. Researchers using radiocarbon dating methods to study tree growth in the world's largest tropical rainforest have found that 50% of all trees greater than 10 centimetres (4inches) in diameter are more than 300 years old. Some of the trees are 750 to 1,000 years old. The slow growing nature of the Amazon trees in fact mean that it takes longer for the forest to recover from logging. It may take centuries for the rainforest to grow to its full size after deforestation.

The diversity of the trees that form the canopy is astounding. Some trees have broad spherical canopies, while others are spindly. One tree species has a high, narrow trunk with a deep green bush at the top. Much of the vegetation drapes into the river.

Visitors take home fond memories of the huge trees and the wildlife and not so fond memories of the large population of ants, chippers and mosquitoes. As a visitor you observe the incredible diversity of life that occurs when the equatorial rainforest is allowed to flourish undisturbed. This is especially true for the more easily seen animals living in these tall trees. Some wildlife such as the jaguar, the peccary and the tapir, is mostly nocturnal, and a visitor will not be able to observe them unless special arrangements are made ahead of time.

We need to know why we must preserve the rainforests. The world's rainforests are ecosystems with a delicate balance of life; they are home to an amazing number of medicinal plants and organisms, and the Amazon basin is no exception. As the rainforest species disappear, so do many possible cures for life-threatening diseases. Think of this for a moment: currently 121 prescription drugs sold worldwide come from plant-derived sources, 25% of Western medical ingredients are derived from the rainforest, but less than 1% of the tropical vegetation has been tested by pharmacologists. If the Amazon rainforest is properly cared for, all known diseases might have a cure. No more cancer. No more AIDS. Malaria can be treated using the bark from the cinchona tree, which contains quinine. Possibly future generations will develop new ways to combat diseases. So, you and I need to protect and save the rainforests of the entire world.

Generally speaking, the reserved area surrounding any official visitors Canopy Walkway are well-preserved by the people operating the visitors' facilities. The forest floor is green from the ground to the canopy, moss covers the tree trunks, and plants upon plants are hanging from every bit of bark. Everywhere you look tiny bird nests are built into the trunks and in the branches. Birds hoot from the canopy, but it is difficult to spot them from the forest floor through the thick canopy.

The forest floor is covered in thick greenery, undisturbed by roads, houses, even human figures. It is then that you realise the legacy of the Amazon rainforest. Visitors are permitted to walk on well-preserved paths, in order for the forest to be left to its own devices. The marked walking paths are easy to follow, and if you time your walk carefully you can have a path all to yourself. You can enjoy the areas of the forest floor beneath the canopy because they are examples of harmonious pristine ecosystems. If you treat the canopy trees with respect, you are paying homage to Mother Nature. In a short distance, a visitor can see banana, plantain, starfruit, lime, mahogany, guayaba, and many other trees and plants.

A visitor may come upon a large metal or wooden construction vaguely resembling a scaffold tower, with lookout points facing the longest view of the canopy. Be careful! The rainforest climate can have a detrimental effect on wooden or metal structures. Some steps or wooden planks may be loose, hinges may give way or parts of the top platform may be rusted.

Many visitors take guided Canopy Walkway tours, which are excellent for spotting animals living in the lush canopy. This of course does not leave much space for personal contact with nature. But you must remember that the Amazon rainforest is not a fairytale land—your personal safety is of the utmost importance.

Canopy Walkways are long, suspended bridges. Most are a series of suspended bridges connected with each other by observation platforms. These observation platforms are secured to canopy trees. There is no sound except the wind and the occasional flock of birds. You are standing on the deep-green roof of the rainforest devoid of any other of human presence.

Professional operators of Canopy Walkways have a direct interest in protecting the environment because ecological tourism provides the best alternative income to logging or farming of the land. Eco-tourism supports both conservation and economic development of the rainforest in a non-destructive manner. Operators are regarded as guardians of the Amazon. The alternative is grim. Through logging of tall trees, we are losing Earth's greatest biological treasures just as we are beginning to appreciate their true value. Rainforests once covered 15% of the earth's surface; now they cover a mere 5% and at this rate of deforestation, the future does not look promising.

Short-sighted governments, multi-national corporations and greedy land owners are logging the rainforest because they perceive the value to lie only in its timber. Forests are clear-cut by chainsaws, bulldozers, and charcoal-makers. This is then followed by farming and ranging operations, and then followed by oil drilling.

Protection of the environment and in particular, protection of the support trees used for canopy walkways is of primary concern to visitors and operators. Care must be taken by both operators and visitors so as not to require the removal of any limbs or large branches, and extremely minimal pruning should be done to the surrounding canopy trees. In the design used to build canopy walkways, neither the suspended bridges nor the platforms should be nailed or bolted to the trees. A well-maintained canopy walkway should be safe for visitors and both the material and design should be chosen to meet maximum standards.

The starting point of a canopy walkway is normally located atop of the highest hill in the area. From there, the suspended bridge goes out at a slight grade, quickly climbing into the top of the tallest canopy trees. The average height is more than 40 meters (120 feet) above the forest floor.

With unprecedented access to the lush canopy, the suspended walkways provide a wonderful opportunity to observe and study the rich plant and animal diversity. It is a unique opportunity for western school groups and can be an effective educational tool for getting students interested in learning all about the Amazon rainforest. The research potential is huge as well. On a more personal level, a trip to an Amazon canopy walkway builds the visitor's spirit of adventure.

The Amazon Exploration Series   *Constantine Issighos*

Amazonian Canopy: The Roof of the World's Rainforest

The Amazon Exploration Series *Constantine Issighos*

Amazonian Canopy: The Roof of the World's Rainforest

The Amazon Exploration Series *Constantine Issighos*

Amazonian Canopy: The Roof of the World's Rainforest

Amazonian Canopy: The Roof of the World's Rainforest

The Amazon Exploration Series *Constantine Issighos*

Amazonian Canopy: The Roof of the World's Rainforest

The Amazon Exploration Series   *Constantine Issighos*

Amazonian Canopy: The Roof of the World's Rainforest   25

The Amazon Exploration Series *Constantine Issighos*

Amazonian Canopy: The Roof of the World's Rainforest

The Amazon Exploration Series *Constantine Issighos*

Amazonian Canopy: The Roof of the World's Rainforest

The Amazon Exploration Series *Constantine Issighos*

Amazonian Canopy: The Roof of the World's Rainforest

Amazonian Canopy: The Roof of the World's Rainforest

The Amazon Exploration Series   *Constantine Issighos*

Amazonian Canopy: The Roof of the World's Rainforest

Constantine Issighos *The Amazon Exploration Series*

42 *Amazonian Canopy: The Roof of the World's Rainforest*

The Amazon Exploration Series *Constantine Issighos*

Amazonian Canopy: The Roof of the World's Rainforest

The Amazon Exploration Series *Constantine Issighos*

Amazonian Canopy: The Roof of the World's Rainforest

www.ingramcontent.com/pod-product-compliance
Lightning Source LLC
Chambersburg PA
CBHW041754040426
42446CB00001B/30